PICK-UP ARTISTS'
SECRETS

(Essential Beginner's Guide)

By

Pickup Artists Anonymous

Copyright 2009 – Pickup Artists Anonymous

Disclaimer:

This book provides suggestions only and how the reader uses it is their choice. The authors / publishers are not liable for inappropriate use of the information by the reader.

CONTENTS

Chapter 9: Progression to Sex – Page 116

Chapter 10: Miscellaneous Topics – Page 131

10.12. Checklist for PUAs

Final Thoughts – Page 150

Chapter 1

Introduction to PUA Lifestyle

Pickup Art means the act of enticing and persuading a woman to surrender her chastity (have sex with you!)

You want to enter the Secret world of Pick-Up Artists. You like sex and want more sex with more women – correct? Then be assured that you have got the right book for the Beginner. It is written by a group of Pickup Artists called Pick-Up Artists Anonymous (PUAA). It has all the essential tips, ideas, advice and guidance which we as a group called the PUAA could find - all in one spot explained in a simple step by step manner. No more reading through the non-essential fluff of tons of PUA books. This is the only book which you need to read, re-read and understand so that you can begin your journey. We have done all the essential research, analysis, experimentation, studied the masters, and eventually found out what works with women. In short we have done the hard work and this is the one reference book you will ever need to get started. What we have learnt is that you don't have to be incredibly rich, famous or have amazing looks to get laid. But you do need to know the key secrets of the 'Game'. Pick-Up Artistry has its own set of 'rules' and you need to know them to score the winning points (have sex!). Let's face facts - the truth is that most guys live at the whims of women because they do not know how to play the Game to Win. This pocket size book will guide you with all the essential information minus the useless fluff on how to become a Pickup Artist (PUA). We have put in a lot of effort to write this book and we do believe this is the best possible guide for any Beginner.

Enjoy Life to the Max as it is short!

1.1. The Game

In Pick-Up Artist's (PUA) world 'Game' means the

ability to fulfill one's desire for women and sex. The goal is to Win the Game, and also enjoy the process of playing. It is about developing the skills and mindset to become good with the opposite sex.

1.2. PUA

A Pick-Up Artist (PUA) is a male who has committed himself to studying and applying the art of pickup and seduction of women in order to maximize fulfillment of his sexual desires.

1.3. PUAA

Pick-Up Artists Anonymous is a fellowship of men who share their knowledge and experience with each other so that they can have more sex with more women. Through this book we offer suggestions only but we do not tell you what you should or should not do.

1.4. PUA Communities

PUA Communities are fast growing and can be found in almost every part of the world. They are also known as Seduction Societies. Most of the members lead a private life for obvious reasons. However they do get together online or offline to help each other by sharing experiences and information. You can find out more about your nearest PUA community by searching the Internet forums.

1.5. Basic Steps of Becoming a PUA

1. Understanding psychology of women
2. Inner game – improve confidence and develop personality
3. Outer game – improve appearance and become fashionable
4. Playing the Game to Win

1.6. What it takes to be a PUA

To execute the knowledge that is given to you in this book it needs a few key elements in you:

- You have to be a man with a burning desire for sex with women – more and more sex.
- You have to have dedication, passion, time and patience.
- You have to believe in trial and error, learn to experiment and see what works for you. .
- You have to be willing to be rejected as you go through this process and forgive yourself for your mistakes.

1.6. Conclusion

This is not rocket science but you need to be dedicated in your pursuit of Women and Sex. Also remember like most things in life you will only get out what you have put in and if things are not working out for you as you are then you must be honest with yourself and modify your techniques.

Chapter 2
Basics of Pick-Up Art

2.1. AFC Versus PUA

There are basically two categories of men in the PUA world. One type is called the Average Frustrated Chump (AFC). The other type is the PUA. The AFC is the typical modern male who has had some (minimal) success with women mostly by chance. By and large AFC is clueless about what it takes to sexually attract a woman. On the other hand PUA is a student of the seduction process. He has committed himself to studying and applying the art of pickup and seduction for sex.

2.2. Understanding Women

Women think differently to men. Often they have a certain generalized pattern in which they think and act while dealing with men. It is influenced largely by the standards of society. For the PUA it is important to understand this in order to manipulate them.

- Women are very sensitive and are always concerned about their reputation. To sleep with many men is generally considered a shameful act for any woman.

- Women have sexual needs but her emotional connection needs are linked with it. She wants to be cherished and appreciated as it makes her feel more desirable and beautiful.

- Women are afraid of being hurt, they are taught to believe that men can be a threat to them.

So basically on the one hand she wants love and affection from men and on the other hand she is fearful of damaging her reputation (people calling her slut) or hurting her self-esteem. This fear can come across as coldness or snobbishness. Your job as PUA is to learn how you can go past her defenses discretely. This book will give you all the essential knowledge by which you can influence her and win the Game! It needs practice to perfect the Art. The best way to do that is to talk to women wherever you go. The more you talk to them, the more you will learn about their way of thinking and this will help you to develop your social skills. Also remember scoring is a number (volume) game, so you need to make as many attempts at possible. You need to be resilient to rejection and not take it personally. More attempts will eventually lead to more sex.

2.3. Inner Game

This is the area of the game that deals with your state of mind. Your Inner Game is the key to your success. It is those things which you have to generate from inside. This includes five things:

- Attitude
- Self-confidence
- Self-esteem
- Self-talk
- Personality

2.3.1. Attitude about Yourself

This attitude of being true to yourself is attractive to women. If you can show that you are positive about your own abilities and your strengths, the women you meet will like you more. If you have goals, take responsibility of your life and have a balanced approach to life, these will demonstrate your attractiveness to women. Learn to be calm in the face of distress – by being patient and forgiving of yourself and others. People become stressed only when they lose patience and start reacting impulsively. Have a dream for your future and show it in your actions. All these are 'words' which will turn women on. Let them know about your positive attitude towards life and this will show them that you are not just another average guy.

2.3.2. Self-confidence

Self-confidence is the difference between feeling unstoppable with Women and feeling scared out of your wits. Your perception of yourself has an enormous impact on how women perceive you. The more self-confidence you have, the more likely it is you'll succeed. Make a list of your strengths and qualities. Avoid comparing yourself with others and accept yourself wholeheartedly. Look at yourself honestly as a capable and fulfilling person, not dependent on approval or acceptance from others. Write down all the qualities that make you a likable person. Then whenever you're faced with a situation where you're not feeling confident, just recite the list (called affirmation technique) about your positive qualities in your mind. Always have an upbeat attitude and try to be 'your best'. Be a positive man who women can enjoy being around. What's true is even when you 'fake' a confident personality, you'll eventually develop this personality trait! Before you approach women, have a plan of action. This little mental preparation will go a long way towards building your self-confidence.

2.3.3. Self-esteem

Men who have poor self-esteem tend to focus on and magnify their perceived shortcomings, and ignore their strengths and achievements. In order to be having a healthy self-esteem you need to like yourself. If you believe that 'you are not OK', or if you are constantly putting yourself down, you are more likely to feel depressed, anxious or miserable than someone who has a positive view of themselves. Your self-esteem will influence the way you behave with other women. You will be afraid to express your views, because you would be scared of rejection all the time. Also you will appear as desperate and needy which will turn women away from you.

2.3.4. Self-talk

A good way to build your self-esteem is to become your own best friend. Change your self-talk. This means talking to yourself in the same supportive way that you would talk to your best friend – with kindness and fairness. You need to see yourself in a balanced way, and not focus on or exaggerate your perceived flaws. Everyone is a mixture of good and bad. Challenge your negative inner self-talk by logically arguing against it in your mind. Use affirmations (motto) like "I am a prize and women will be enriched by my presence". Repeat this throughout the day and especially when approaching a woman and starting to play the Game. Write it down in your room at a place where you can see it all the time.

2.3.5. Personality

Women like men with personality. It is those qualities that makes you a distinct individual and conspicuous among other men. Your presence should be such that the women do not feel insecure or threatened. Having empathy towards others can make you more attractive with women. Be warm and encouraging towards others and use words to boost the self-esteem of others. However do not overdo this as it may backfire. Otherwise they may think you are needy and desperate. Women like men who have interests and hobbies. They want to know you have a real life - a life that you actually enjoy. So be prepared with some story in advance to display your personality and carry on an interesting conversation about yourself. Have a working knowledge of the current events in the news. Learn about the latest movies and books. Develop an 'exciting' skill that you can talk about interestingly without boring her. It can only come through practice and trial & error with different topics. Don't however make one of the common mistakes many men do which is focusing the entire conversation on yourself.

Remember a woman becomes interested in you only because of how you make her feel. You want to make her feel like she is exciting and interesting too, so ask about her life. Show a whole range of emotions as you listen to her, including curiosity, fascination, humor and sincerity. Women absolutely love emotions and if you use them in response to her, she will connect to them and to you.

2.3.6. Conclusion

Developing strong Inner Game is the core strength of PUAs. Overcoming one's insecurities and negative thought patterns and projecting confidence in self is the best way to demonstrate high value to women. Most PUAs are happy positive people who have passions outside of Pickup Game and the presence of women in their life makes them happier. They never show signs of being needy or desperate because with or without women, their life is always fulfilling. This is the attitude they project to women.

2.3.7. Checklist

How many of these qualities describe you?

Adventurous	Educated
Attentive to details	Enthusiastic
Charming	Funny
Classy	Happy
Confident	Intelligent
Creative	Passionate
Cultured	Romantic
Dominant	Social
Driven	Thoughtful
	Unpredictable

2.4. Outer Game

The Outer Games refers to those things that are apparent on the outside. This area of the Game is purely technique based. Outer Game eliminates discussions on personality differences and focuses on a PUA's 'outer' reflection of the Game. This includes:

Appearance and clothes   Posture and voice

Health and hygiene   Home environment

2.4.1. Appearance and Clothes

Dressing well says to women that you like yourself and that you enjoy looking good. Always choose clothing that is appealing and tasteful. A casual look can be both comfortable and yet stylish. As a man, you want a stylish haircut that sends the message to women that you care about your appearance. Make sure to trim hair from nose and ears. Also look after your eyebrows and shave or trim excessive body hair. Trim your beard if you have one but otherwise shave properly to give yourself a clean masculine look. Make sure your belt and shoe colors match and keep your shoes clean. Your accessories like watch and sunglasses should be matching your style. Stay in step with the latest male fashions without going overboard. A sloppy or unkempt appearance is not acceptable to any woman.

2.4.2. Health and Hygiene

You do not need to have a muscular body. However you do need to show that you are physically fit. If you find yourself running out of breath when doing simple things like walking up a few stairs or playing catch, it's time to improve your physical condition. Incorporate more physical exercise into your daily routine. Eat healthy and drink more water everyday. Get adequate rest. Good hygiene shows that you care about your appearance. Shower daily to get rid of body odor. Use deodorants and cologne. Keep your mouth clean and see that you do not have a bad breath when you meet women. Make sure you are always looking well groomed. Keep your nails clean.

Clean clothes is another way to upkeep your personal hygiene. Also make sure that undergarments and socks are constantly kept clean and fresh by changing them often (these things do matter when you are a PUA.).

2.4.3. Posture and Voice

In order to be classy and confident you need to practice maintaining good posture. Looking confident doesn't mean strutting around - confidence shows up as a comfortably erect posture without trying too hard. Women know the difference between being over-confident and easy confidence. Men who are confident look into the woman's eyes when they talk to them while those that are not will seem shifty eyed. Confident guys are relaxed, their hands are at the sides or on the table - they don't keep touching themselves or something. They speak clearly and are not too loud or too soft, and generally seem to be clear-headed. Confident men have pleasant relaxed expressions on their face while the guy who is not, seems to have anxious mannerisms. You'll find that confident men are focused on their thoughts and actions. Don't appear nervous when you talk to women. Also try not to smoke before or while meeting her. You may think it makes you look confident, but it doesn't in today's society. And we don't know any woman who loves bad breath, yet! Talking too fast or nonstop is considered irritating. It makes you look uneasy and not in control of yourself. Instead, ask interesting questions, encouraging her to talk more. It makes a great impression when you are a good listener. You will appear more interesting to her when she realizes she's done most of the talking. Confidence has to show from within. So think along those lines, only then will it show in your actions. Your facial expressions will show it, and so will your posture. You will not slouch. Instead you will stand erect and ready for anything, with pleasure. Changing your inner Self-talk always helps. Tell yourself you look fabulous today and feel good about you. It is easier to feel good when you actually do look good, and this is where the self-grooming comes in.

2.4.4. Home Environment

For the PUA who is planning to bring women to his place for sex, this is really important. Your home says something about who you are. So make sure it is making the right statement. Keep it neat, clean and organized. Before you bring her in adjust the temperature so that it is not going to be too cold when you both get naked. Add dim lights, romantic music and fragrance to the atmosphere to make it romantic. Keep the bathroom clean and have a set of extra towels, an extra robe and an extra toothbrush in it for her to use. Keep your bed clean and fresh. Get rid of anything in your home that reminds you of previous girlfriends. Have modern, comfortable furnishings in your home. Consider having conversation pieces like interesting artwork or a piece of furniture, an art easel or guitar. These are items that communicate things about your style and personality. Keep a bottle of

Champagne or wine in the refrigerator. Have some chocolate or strawberries and you will certainly impress her. Turn your phone off and make sure that there are no messages from other women in your answering machine. Keep condoms handy and close to the bed.

2.4.5. Conclusion

The way we think has influence on our behavior and our behavior is what people see as our personality. So the Outer Game is inter-dependent on the way we think of ourselves. (Inner Game of the PUA) The Outer game does influence the Inner Game significantly. The PUA knows that a good Outer Game will give him more confidence. The PUA's body language when approaching women, voice tonality, eye contact, and the conversation opener are all Outer Game related attributes. The good thing about the Outer Game is that it can be developed quickly by using the techniques discussed above.

Chapter 3
Before the Game Begins

3.1. Introduction

In order to be a PUA, one needs to know the difference between Friend Zone (FZ) and Fuck Buddy (FB). He must also learn how to not fall into the friend zone even before he plans to get started.

3.2. Friend Zone (FZ)

The friend zone is where a man ends up with a platonic relationship with a woman but gets no sex. "Let's just be friends" (LJBF) - this is a statement uttered by women that essentially closes the door to a sexual relationship; being put in the Friend Zone. LJBF is a type of rejection but the woman is using kind words to soften the blow because she thinks of him as a 'Nice Guy'. PUAs know how to not enter the FZ by making their sexual intentions clear upfront. They do not waste time chasing after someone who is not interested in him. LJBFs occur usually because an AFC builds too much comfort with a woman, without creating any sexual tension. They do this mistake by focusing too much on one single woman at a time.

3.3. Fuck Buddy (FB)

PUAs are usually interested in casual sexual encounters with many female partners without getting into the trap of commitment. Women who engage in casual sex with PUA are referred to as Fuck Buddy. Although many women may openly condemn this kind of activity, they will often engage in the practice secretly. PUAs take advantage of this fact. PUAs do not rush into exclusive committed relationships, as is common among AFCs.

3.4. Right Attitude

In order to get started, PUAs need to adopt the right attitude of both the Inner and Outer Game. If you are a new student of PUA techniques, first congratulate yourself for deciding to go beyond your comfort zone. Your fear is based on your imagination of some negative outcome. PUAs do not think of the outcome. They enjoy the process of learning. Even while playing they do not know what the outcome of the Game will be. They know how to give it a good shot and enjoy the process of learning. However this commitment to learning is their strength. They accept their fear as natural and use their knowledge of the Inner and Outer Game to overcome it. When they approach women, they know how to demonstrate their Value by using a warm body language and communication skills (which we will teach discuss later on in this book). This type of positive attitude in the PUA will make him more attractive that the AFC. It will generate the Approach Invitation from women.

3.5. Approach Invitation (AI)

PUAs are always searching for the Approach Invitation (AI) from women at every venue. When they walk into a social situation where there are Targets (women), they observe the venue to scan for women who display the AI signals. These are subtle non-verbal signals that women give to show that they are interested in being approached by the man. Most women do this without being obvious, as they do not want to feel like a slut.

3.6. AI Signals

These are Indicators of Interest (IOI) shown by women. It means she wants to be approached. The most common AI signals include frequent eye contact and smile. Here is a list of commonly used AI.

- Compliments you
- Initiates conversation
- Introduces you to her friends

- Licks her lips

- Looks at you from the corner of her eye

- Moves her body towards you

- Repeatedly glances at you

- Sits up straighter, thrusting out her boobs

- Smiles and giggles

- Tips her head

- Touches her hair or clothing

- Touches you

- You find her coincidentally around you

3.7. Indicators of Interest (IOI)

These are the conscious and unconscious signs of interest shown by women. The PUA is always keenly observant and notes her body language while speaking with her. Depending on these, the PUA decides to proceed accordingly. The usual ones are holding eye contact, touching her hair, leaning towards the PUA, touching

PUA, complying with a request, saying something to complement PUA, licking her lips, pushing her breasts forward, willing to leave the venue with PUA etc. Sometimes women who are manipulative can also use 'false' IOI to get some favor from men.

3.8. Indicators of Disinterest (IOD) / Not Interested Signals

The PUA also knows how to read the signs conveying disinterest. They can be verbal such as a woman telling a PUA "that's not funny" or "I have a boyfriend"; or it can be physical, like avoiding eye contact and evasive body language. Non-verbal IODs tend to be more reliable than just words. However sometimes women can test the genuineness of the PUA by showing IOD. So experienced PUAs may try to explore her IOD before moving on to another target. Some ways to overcome IODs are by either Negging (explained later) or doing a False Takeaway. If the IOD is coming from the Target's girlfriend then the PUA must recognize the need to win her approval first before he can isolate the Target. Here is a list of IOD.

- Acts defensive
- Acts like a bitch
- Appears completely disinterested
- Avoids eye contact
- Leans away from you
- No sense of humor
- Points out her wedding ring
- Says she has a boyfriend
- Sits in a hard to reach spot
- Surrounds herself with her friends
- Uses negative body language

3.9. False Takeaway

PUA makes the Target think that he is leaving the venue

making her chase him in order for him to stay. This can be verbal (saying that he is leaving) or non-verbal (physical movement suggestive that he is about to leave).

3.10. Peacocking

Peacocking is the technique used by some PUAs to get attention of females in busy environments like nightclubs where there is lot of competition. It is usually some showy accessory (like hat, necklace etc.) worn by the PUA which can encourage women to start conversation by commenting on the article. It also shows that the PUA has a unique attitude and can deal with any type of social pressure by being exclusive and yet confident.

3.10. Conclusion

Becoming a PUA is all about learning the real and effective rules in the seduction Game. Firstly be Positive about your Self Game (Inner + Outer). Secondly, never quit learning. Thirdly be prepared to accept Rejection. There are billions of women on the planet just waiting to date with you. Generally PUAs believe that shame on those women that have lost the opportunity to know him better. Fourthly make an action plan for your own Game and try to be proactive. Lastly do not give up easily, slowly you will find your Game improving. To be a successful PUA you must learn to believe that all women are dispensable and replaceable. PUAs never think of sticking with one woman unlike the AFCs.

Chapter 4

PUA Personality Types

4.1. Introduction

There are different types of PUA personalities. Each has its own merit and demerit. What works for you depends on your style and dedication. Dedication involves time, effort and persistence. This is common to all types of PUAs.

4.2. The Alpha Male

He is the leader amongst the men. He stands out because of his attitude. He creates a cool sexy vibe by displaying dominant, masculine behavior. He is comfortable and content with himself and doesn't depend on anyone else to tell him 'who he is'.

4.2.1. Personal Attributes

Becoming an Alpha Male is like learning any other skill -it takes a great amount of learning, observing, imitating, practicing and determination.

- Busy at all times: They do not have time to waste, do not leave messages on phone or sit on hold. Instead the Alpha Male asks her to call back when she's got the time to focus on him.
- Self-interested: Engaged with his own goals in life, not self-centered, but makes sure he knows what is important for him. His goals come first. He comes across as having fun with his own goals in life.
- Responsible: The Alpha Male demonstrates through the actions that he is proactive and takes responsibility of his life and his actions.
- Intelligence: Shows that he is intelligent and smart

in his thinking. Dominance in his character is by using intelligence and not physical force.

- Independent: Lives by his own rules, does not seek approval from others including women.
- Softer side: Has a gentle emotional side and shows it appropriately. Is generous without any expectations.
- Goal: Has his own goals in life and works towards fulfilling them with passion and persistence.
- Adventurous: Is wiling to take chances and explore the potential within him.
- Forgiving: Of self and others, knows when to let go and move on. Does not go around apologizing to others for his behavior.
- Eager to learn. He shows interest in self-development.
- Optimistic and flexible. Does not give up when failure strikes. Readjusts his beliefs and keeps persisting.
- Balanced: Lives life in moderation and knows

when to draw the line.

- Willing to put women second: His own life goals are more important to him than women.

- Humorous: Able to laugh at self and the world. He does not laugh at the expense of others or uses vulgar topics to promote his sense of humor. Able to debate with women using humor. Helps her feel good with original creative compliments and not cheesy pickup lines.

- Time conscious and yet patient. Values time and acts now. Does not wait for tomorrow. However when it comes to women, he does not show any sign of impatience.

- Knows how to show his best qualities to women. Demonstrates his powerfulness to women by proving that he is an expert in his area of knowledge.

- Follows his own code of honor. Lives by his own code of ethics, values and principles.

- Maintains a calm mysterious appearance. Does not

reveal his cards, keeps the woman guessing.

4.2.2. Develop a Code of Honor

"A break from the norm" perfectly describes an Alpha Male. To the Alpha Male everything he does in life centers around his own personal code of ethics, beliefs and values. He demonstrates to female targets that his life centers around these core values. Example:

- Loyalty, love and respect to your parents and other family members
- Courageous and brave, patient and honorable, sincere and honest, respectful of others
- Ability to be hard and cool, soft and compassionate, always in control
- Good manners / etiquette

Examples: James Bond (Sean Connery), George Clooney, Richard Burton, Antonio Banderas, Brad Pitt, Russell

Crowe.

4.2.3. Beta Male

He is the exact opposite of the Alpha Male. He uses excuses to comfort his shortcomings. Does not like taking risks and avoids confrontation with females. He comes across as a weak personality. He has poor self-esteem and thinks that he does not get women because he is too short / fat / ugly / poor / stupid / shy / boring, etc. Make sure that you are not being a Beta Male by getting rid of anything you connect to old girlfriends, any depressive music, any clothes which make you feel uncomfortable, emotional baggage from previous relationships etc.

4.2.4. Conclusion

If you believe in yourself strongly enough, the judgments of others become completely irrelevant. This includes woman's opinions, by the way. An Alpha Male does not define his value by what any woman thinks of him. He believes in himself — and others automatically follow him.

4.3. Mind Reader

This is the type of PUA personality which uses Neuro-Linguistic Programming (NLP), or to put it simply - techniques of subtle suggestions to influence her subconscious thinking and creating an emotional connection. It was introduced by Ross Jeffries. He suggested use of language patterns, embedded commands, story telling and behavior techniques like anchoring etc. to seduce women and have sex. He also suggested use of NLP to change the Inner Game by using it to improve PUAs inner attitude and overcome fear.

4.3.1. Use of NLP on the PUA (Self NLP)

NLP seduction can help a person realize his self-worth and change his inner belief. He can get rid of his negative thoughts about approaching women and about seduction. He can use NLP to create positive affirmations in himself to gain confidence.

4.3.2. Use of NLP on Women (Targets)

NLP seduction uses suggestive language to slowly change her perception about having sex and relax her defenses to be intimate with the PUA.

4.3.3. Controversy

The use of NLP seduction is actually controversial. Some experts claim that it is actually a great breakthrough. Others however suggest being cautious in using it. It is particularly noteworthy that NLP, as a system in itself, has never been truly scientifically approved. Some men also dismiss the system and prefer instead to go for the other traditional seduction approaches.

4.3.4. Steps of NLP techniques

Positive use of language: A simple but effective use of NLP is to make sure you never use negative language. Saying "today wasn't amazing, things didn't go as perfectly as I'd imagined" is better than "today was awful, things went terribly". Just simply using positive words rather than negative words allows you to convey the same information without affecting the mood.

Pacing and leading: If she is speaking negatively, first pace it by agreeing and expanding on it, but then take charge and turn things positive by changing the subject or positively re-framing the negative event. Pacing and leading also applies to energy and state. If she is cold with you, don't be loving with her, instead match her coldness and then slowly lead her into being seductive by slowly becoming seductive yourself. The same applies to if she is tired or bored, pace and then lead.

Mirroring and matching: When people spend a lot of time together, they tend to share mannerisms, reactions, vocabulary, tone and speed of speech. You can see this with good friends, couples, and relatives. If you match and mirror someone, they will feel a lot more comfortable and relaxed with you as if they have known you longer. Do this by speaking at a similar speed, and using a similar amount of gestures. Feeding back the same words they use in conversation. Mirroring the way they sit, the amount of cyc contact, and the facial expression. You can actually get away with a surprising amount of mirroring and matching – most women don't seem to notice!

Anchoring: Anchoring is the process of linking a touch, sound, or visual input to an emotion. When the woman laughs, you can click your fingers, or touch her and it will anchor the emotion to the click or touch. Later you can try to re-trigger the emotion by simply firing the anchor -

the touch or click. You can also anchor by playing songs when she is with you that she will later hear and associate to being with you.

Patterns: NLP patterns for seduction involve the use of language to bring out an emotion in the girl that is desirable given the current circumstances. An example of an NLP seduction pattern would be: "Have you ever just met someone and almost immediately you start to feel <u>incredibly comfortable</u> like you've known this person forever and then as you just let the barriers drop and you let them more inside you start to naturally feel a sense of rightness, like <u>this is meant to be</u>". For greater effect, the underlined words should be "marked out" by delivering them with vocal variety and passion.

Storytelling: Another example that uses NLP is to introduce sexual ideas through the use of story telling. If you want her thinking about fantastic sex with a stranger in a bar (namely you), tell the story of this guy you met last week who had fantastic sex with a girl he met in a bar. If you want her to think about how much you'd love a blow job, tell a story about some 'tacky' guy who you work with who came up to a girl in a bar and asked her for one right out loud. As you both chuckle at his outright stupidity, what is she thinking about? Blow jobs.

4.3.5. Conclusion

NLP can be a powerful tool of influence for any PUA. To land the woman of your dreams you will need to experiment with all the available tools at your disposal to maximize your chances.

4.4. Grand Master (GM)

This is an advanced PUA approach, which needs a lot of courage, but the effects can be quick. The GM style is blatantly sexual and forward, in a confident and unapologetic manner. The GM style approach can work well or not work depending on a PUA's personality. GM style takes an extraordinary amount of self-control and an outgoing personality, allowing the PUA to keep talking and take a lot of Shit Tests from women without losing his cool.

4.4.1. GM techniques

In a nutshell, GM approach involves the PUA first telling the woman blatantly that he wants to fuck her. He uses dirty sex jokes and continuous humorous sex-talk with keen attention to how the Target reacts. If she is likely to show negative reaction, he prevents it by saying, "just kidding", giving an "apologetic" hug to the girl etc. Then, follow that right up with as many sexual jokes as you can think of, then another sexual innuendo like before. The point is to not even give her a chance to respond before she is laughing and having fun with you. A key to remember is that once you have started down this road, there is no putting it in reverse. You have to keep up the patter and not let her get in a word edgewise. To make sure this works, you will have to memorize one-liners and jokes so that you do not run out. For material, go online or get dirty joke books. This is an aggressive style. The PUA has to show the attitude that he could satisfy these women sexually. He had the confidence that says he does this all the time. He is in their face. He makes them excited. He keeps stimulating them like they are not used to being stimulated. If they were going to resist, they would have resisted when he first told them what he wanted from them. The GM approach makes the assumption that women like dick, they love it and they want it! The problem is they want it from the guys they want it from. All he has to do is offer them the next best thing...sexual satisfaction as opposed to sex with a man they want! He doesn't even have to satisfy them. It's too late by the time he's fucking them! All he has to do is make them believe that if they get with him he is going to fuck them well! They would not resist because at some point they will become horny and want that release of sexual tension.

4.4.2. Conclusion

This GM technique will cause one of two things to happen. She will either walk away angrily, meaning she wasn't the one you wanted in the first place or she will laugh and you two will hit it off because she can see that you are a dominant, confident and honest man.

4.5. Bad Boy

In PUA societies, the Bad Boy refers to dominant males who have unpredictable, non-conformist traits. He is inattentive to women, arrogant and independent. He plays hard to get, uses an almost uninterested attitude towards women. He shows impulsiveness, is fond of thrill seeking, promiscuous behavior. He is insensitive and deceitful towards women. He puts himself first and does what he wants when he wants. He treats women as replaceable and as such makes them work hard to get his attention. He is able to remain cool under pressure, has a rebellious attitude to life and is recklessly adventurous. He treats women badly and uses them for sex.

4.5.1. Bad Boy Approach

The best example would be rock and roll stars. Most women know these guys are surrounded by beautiful women. But they still line up in the hundreds and thousands just to be near them. Well a lot of it has to do with the 'bad boy' attitude they project. These dudes know how to cultivate a specific personality that makes women crazy with desire. You can do that by projecting a confident and relaxed attitude under any situation. Never fall for a woman's Shit Tests. Women test guys all the times. The reason they do this is to see how much they can manipulate men and control their actions. Whenever she tries to create drama or force you to do something, you either ignore her requests or simply call her out on her actions. Never show your weakness for her. Instead you behave in a manner where you're in control. If you want to do something nice for her, you do it on your terms, not hers. Act like you don't care about hooking up when you're talking to her. What's great about this attitude is you appear to be different to the other men who spend the majority of their time making overt attempts to seduce women. While they wine and dine women, you spend time enjoying their company, but not 'putting the moves' on them. By acting like you don't care, you'll look like a prize she has to obtain. One of the basic principles in psychology is how people always want what they can't have. By creating an aloof, 'I don't care' attitude, you'll make her work for your affections. As a result, she'll be chasing after you instead of the other way around. Let women know that your life is exciting and you like to take risks and have adventures. You can do this by using interesting stories or having some uncommon hobby. Women don't want a guy they can walk all over. Nodding patiently, going out of your way to impress them, and backing off when someone treats you inappropriately - these are the things most women just can't stand. You're acting like you're less than them, and there's just no challenge there! Project qualities like confidence, adventure, popularity but also let her know that you are able to protect her when needed. Be the guy who straps her in her seat belt on the roller coaster, or who offers a hand so that she doesn't trip. Trust is built upon these actions. By doing the little things for her, like walking on the part of the sidewalk between her and the street, or keeping an eye open for anything potentially dangerous, or standing up for her immediately when anyone attacks her verbally or physically, she'll learn to trust that you, indeed, have a Bad Boy within you ready to stand up for her and defend her if necessary. Let her know that you find her sexually attractive. Drop hints that will intrigue her. Say something risky, and grin when her mouth drops. They may act shocked, even offended, but actually they love it when you tease them. Don't let anyone walk over you. Show that you don't care what others say or think. No matter how a woman reacts, it just blows right over you. That's because you're always in control. No woman - whether beautiful, popular, or rich-has power over you. You don't need anyone, you're not dependent on anyone, and you don't have to cling to anyone. Act like her protector but at the same time stand up for yourself. Develop that attitude which says you've got the power to do whatever you want. You'll be irresistible to women in no time!

4.5.2. Conclusion

The Bad Boy has an attitude closely aligned with the Alpha Male but he is a non-conformist and rebellious. Just as we are turned on by a woman's femininity, masculinity turns on women. To begin with say something unexpected out of the ordinary to startle her, chat nicely briefly and then walk away. This will intrigue her. Women love challenges. The Bad Boy poses a challenge as he cannot be tamed easily like other men. They've already turned down all the men who have groveled and begged for their attention; you are something all new. So if you're a Bad Boy be assured that there are a ton of women who want nothing more than a Bad Boy!

4.6. Cocky & Funny (C+F)

This type of PUA uses a mix of cockiness (confidence) and a sense of humor, modeled from the behavior of typical 'Bad Boys'. He believes in the number (volume) Game and does not take rejections personally. He uses humor to create attraction and balances out his arrogance. It also helps him to build rapport by using flirtatious teasing and banter. His cockiness makes him less needy where as his humor makes him more attractive. In C+F the PUAs key style is fearless approach, pursuing many women at the same time and considering every encounter as a prospect for sex. He is persistent and his personality is enjoyable because of his sense of humor. He believes that focusing on one woman is risky business as it will make him dependent on her to maintain his self-esteem.

4.7. Summary

Alpha Male – develop attractive commanding personality style to get women

Mind-reader – use Neuro-linguistic Programming (NLP) mental influencing techniques to seduce.

Grand Master – uses assertiveness and bold approach

Bad Boy – uses casual uninterested reverse behavior approach

Cocky Funny – uses cocky humor and confidence

Chapter 5

Approaching Targets (Women)

5.1. Introduction

The Game begins with the approach from the PUA. To have the best approach is the key to success. However it takes time to become a natural expert. Before that it is important to have the right mental preparation (Inner Game) to overcome the fear (aka Approach Anxiety).

5.2. Approach Anxiety (AA)

AA is natural and it can be a result of poor past experiences with women, multiple rejections, sensitivity or shyness, or even cultural factors. However with knowledge of seduction techniques, advance preparation and lots of practice PUAs learn to overcome this fear and eventually toughen up. Often they have their own mental checklist that they go through to optimize their approach.

Most PUAs do not use alcohol to reduce anxiety, as they know many women prefer to stay away from drunken guys. The PUAs knows his goal is essentially to pick up women for sex only. They know that when a woman rejects them, in reality it means she is only rejecting the approach and not the whole person.

5.3. Types of PUA Approaches

- Warm approach
- Cold approach

5.3.1. Warm Approach

Warm approach is used when you approach some target woman who is not a complete stranger. Usually, this takes place during social circle meetings, where both the PUA and the woman have a mutual friend in common. That commonality is usually enough to break the ice, and make starting a conversation and a social relationship with her a lot easier than if the PUA had just run into her in the street. These are easy approaches as it is used with women who already have some common connection with the PUA. Just a little bit is enough for any PUA to begin the conversation.

5.3.2. Cold approach

It refers to approaching a woman the PUA has never met and have no known commonality. It is challenging but it can give you a wider choice. However it requires advanced skills and the chances of rejection are much higher. However any successful PUA would need to go through his share of Cold Approaches in order to get to where he is.

5.4. Sarging

It means going out in the field (social venue) with the intent to Pickup women for sex. It is more motivating to go out with other PUA friends (having common goal) than alone. It is good because when PUAs go in groups, it can be easier for the beginner level PUAs to pick up more women with the combined effort of the group members. Moreover they can give each other support.

5.5. Volume Game

PUAs believe in the concept of the Volume Game (aka Number Game) as it provides them the advantage of quantity and freedom of choice. Moreover they are constantly trying to improve their Game and using the Volume Game tactics of approaching as many women as possible in the shortest possible time. By this they can speed up their self learning curve.

5.6. Do and Don't of the Volume Game

All PUAs believe in the High Volume Game (HVG). These are the important Do and Don't of the HVG which they need to follow to deal with rejection.

- DO NOT take rejection personally.
- DO NOT give up. (Persistence is essential.)

- DO learn from the experience.
- DO remember this is a volume game.

5.7. PUAA Tips to Improve Your Chances

- Observe your own non-verbal clues like body language and posture. Do not lean towards her as it shows that you are anxious, desperate and seeking approval. Let her lean towards you, you need to sit back and appear relaxed.
- Do not ask for permission when you want to escalate the closeness. It shows that you are lacking in confidence and will appear as weak and apologetic. Instead of asking, just do it and see what happens.

- Introduce yourself with an emotional or humorous living story about yourself that demonstrates your personality and core values without being brag. Introduce it in the conversation by saying – that reminds me of when....

- When referring to women, use terms like cute or alright. Do not get into the habit of describing women as hot especially in front of other women. It sends subconscious messages to women that you are either a predator or is desperate for women.

- Practice approaching in Volumes and getting rejected as often as possible. This is what all PUAs have done to learn the tricks of the trade – because that is the only way to success.

- Be careful not to use defensive body language like crossed arms or hands in your pockets as it will give subtle negative signals to women. Be warm and interactive with everyone around to demonstrate your confidence.

- Avoid direct answers as it makes you appear as a

people pleaser. Instead appear mysterious by evading her questions with humor or using counter questions jokingly. Doing the opposite of AFC is the hook to catch her.

5.8. Three Second Rule

This is a technique common with most PUAs to overcome Approach Anxiety (AA). It means to approach the target woman within three seconds of seeing her or her seeing the PUA. The PUAs know that hesitation will only cause more fear. The more time they have to think, the more they may feel nervous. Being spontaneous is also attractive to women. Most PUAs usually approach women with a casual smile or a 'Hi'. This shows their friendly face and demonstrates their social comfort. Then they use different pattern of Openers to grab the Target's attention. Even experienced PUAs keep practicing constantly as they know that if they do not practice, their fear will come back and they will not get laid as frequently as they need!

5.9. Gimmicks

These are attention grabbing tricks used by PUAs. Also these are great to break the ice. Here are few of the common ones.

- Dogs: Walk around with a cute dog or puppy in the park and see how women notice you.
- Babies: They will get more attention any time. Borrow your nephew and take him to the mall and then act helpless.
- Magic tricks: Can be a great ice-breaker with women, most women like to be entertained.
- Handwriting analysis: All of your predictions should be positive and flirtatious.
- Something unconventional: Walk around in public carrying a tall teddy bear, a dozen balloons or a giant heart full of chocolate candy. Women are often

attracted to flowers, balloons, stuffed animals and so on. They ask what is going on - and the conversation begins.

5.10. Conclusion

To become a successful PUA one needs to approach women continuously. He needs to learn from his mistakes and find out by trial and error what works best for him. Sexual connection comes through emotional connection. Successful PUAs use flexible strategies depending on the circumstances.

Chapter 6
Game Opener

6.1. Introduction

Game Opener is the opening words used by the PUA to initiate contact with the target woman or group. It can be a statement, question, or a story to lure her into conversation.

6.2. Indirect Opener

Indirect openers are used without revealing the PUA's true intent. They are usually perceived as neutral harmless casual topics. The objective is to get her attention. They are effective as most people are open to conversations. They also do not put the PUA under direct risk of rejection. Slowly the PUA can work towards building attraction by demonstrating his personality. It is however a slow process and the PUA may end up wasting a lot of time beating around the bush.

6.3. Direct Opener

These are opening lines that directly convey interest to the woman. They work best when the PUA has a Higher Value (like great looks or fame) than the target woman and by default she is already attracted to the PUA. However when used on strangers, it is quite ineffective in many cases. However the success of this type of Opener also depends on how genuine and fearless the PUA sounds. Example: "Hi.... I think you look cute. I want to get to know you better."

6.4. Canned Opener

These are memorized and practiced openers that the PUA uses repeatedly on different women. Often used by new PUAs, they are similar to pick-up lines. They need to be strong and unique to grab the Targets attention. Example,

"My little sister says men lie more…. let me get a second opinion, who do you think lies more?"

6.5. Compliment Opener

This is a type of Direct Opener using a genuine and unique complement. If the woman senses that the complement is unoriginal then she will think you are needy or desperate. Example: "Hi. You are beautiful. Can I buy you a drink?" is a very cheesy Direct Opener most likely to fail. On the other hand a creative Complement Opener like "You look very interesting, and I love that your shoes match the color of your eyes" are more effective.

6.6. Focus Opener

This is a type of Indirect Opener where the PUA starts by talking about something that the woman is already focused on. It is commonly on some topical issue based on the moment in which the PUA finds the woman. They are natural as the PUA in not interrupting her flow of thoughts but rather blending into it. Example, "What do you think of these apples – will they be good?"

6.8. Opinion Opener

It is a type of Indirect Opener where PUAs use some interesting debatable issue to elicit her opinion on the topic. Example, "My girlfriend and I were having a discussion, and we just couldn't come to an agreement – maybe you can help us. Who do you think lies more, men or women?"

6.9. Situational Opener

It is an impromptu opener where the PUA draws her attention on something simple which is going on around them. It is similar to Focus Opener but more generalized. Even Opinion Openers can be considered situational, as long as they are based on something that is going on in the environment.

6.10. Being Playful

Women like to laugh and have fun. So whatever Opener you use, do it without being too nervous or tense. Do what comes naturally to you. Once you have started the conversation look for signs of Indicators of Interest (IOI) on her part.

6.11. Bitch Shicld

It is used to describe a behavior women use when attempting to fend of would-be suitors. Usually in use in clubs, bars, and other pick-up places where women are hit on frequently by men (mostly AFCs). It is important for the PUA to recognize when a Bitch Shield is artificial and when the woman is truly a bitch.

6.12. Shit Test

Shit Test usually refers to those conscious or unconscious tests which women throw at men who approach them to judge their reaction and confidence. It is a way of challenging or disqualifying the potential suitor by giving him a 'hard time'. The PUAs are usually confident and un-flustered by the woman's comments and by this demonstrates their confident attitude and often use humor in response to her comments. They are also known as Congruence Test and are basically used to see if the PUA remains confident under pressure.

6.13. Conclusion

Which is the best approach? It is dependent on the PUAs style. Most experienced PUAs use a mixed style. Main thing is to grab the target woman's attention and open up a conversation. Even when PUAs use memorized openers, they make sure that they appear spontaneous.

Also it is important to stay away from negative topics and keep the mood upbeat.

Chapter 7

The Middle Game - Interaction

7.1. Banter

PUAs use witty and fun style of spoken communication which involves playful teasing which is referred to as Banter. It is about creating a fun experience for the target woman using silly and insignificant topics and playfully mocking each other. In general, it is a good idea to Banter and have fun with everyone in a venue, to raise a PUA's social value and to have a good time.

7.2. Social Proof

Social Proof is a way of demonstrating social value to others. It shows that the PUA is a likeable friendly personality who is fun to be with. In other words he is opposite of a boring person – an entertainer for everyone around. Social Proof need not be real; they only have to be strong evidence of the PUA's perceived value to the Target woman.

7.3. Passive Value

Passive Value in a cold approach often refers to the combination of physical fitness, body language, and natural physical attributes. These are things which are evident but not talked about directly.

7.4. Demonstration of Higher Value (DHV) (Active Value)

This is when the PUA uses a subtle action or a story to increase interest in the target. It could be used to increase the PUAs social value or sometimes it may be used to increase the targets perceived value. Some of the DHV examples would be that other women want you, you have Alpha Male leadership indicators, you are able to protect her, you are able to understand her emotional needs and connect with her or you believe in a cause bigger than your life. It is not the same as bragging, which makes one appear needy. Often PUAs use Wing-man to speak about them for DHV.

7.5. Perceived Value (PV)

The PV refers to the self-judgment with goes on in the mind of the PUA about his own self worth. It can affect his sense of confidence. It can be controlled by mastering a strong Inner and Outer Game that has many characters of DHV. When the PUA feels very confident, his Perceived Value about self increases and it becomes evident in his game.

7.6. Wing-man (Wing)

A trusted fellow friend or PUA who is able and willing to assist the PUA in his pickup goals. Finding good Wing-man can help distract obstacles and DHV of the PUA.

An Obstacle refers to someone who tries to prevent the PUA from progressing with the target. Local pickup groups are good places to meet new Wing-men to go out with.

7.7. Accomplished Introduction (AI)

A well constructed often pre-planned introduction by the PUA of the Wing-man embedded with DHVs for a lasting impression. It is often used to increase credibility of the Wing-man who can use it later to enhance the value of the PUA. It is like – you scratch my back, I scratch yours.

7.8. Hook Point

It means when the Target woman or the group of women starts to show active interest in the PUA and is engaging in communication. The nest step is building rapport.

7.9. Rapport

It depends on building emotional connection gradually. It follows attraction phase. It is based on demonstration of comfort, congruence (similarities) and leads to trust. Emotional Connection (EC) is a combination of strong Inner Game, vulnerability, and trust. For a genuine EC, the connection has to work both ways. It's not a true connection if the PUA share his feelings but the other person holds everything back. For a genuine connection to occur, there usually has to be a slight change in the PUAs feelings towards the woman as well. When developing an emotional connection, it is important not to reveal too much, as it is not the quantity but what matters is the quality of the information which the PUA shares. It is also important to genuinely listen to the woman's words, sub themes, and tonality when creating an EC bond. It is mutual sharing of respect, trust, and a general feeling of being "connected".

7.10. Push and Pull

It is a psychological technique used by the PUA to increase attraction of the Target. The concept is for the PUA to plunge himself in the experience of pulling the girl when it feels good, and then pushing her away, knowing that push will make her want him more, and the return much more rewarding. Push and pull describes the unpredictability and spontaneity of seduction.

7.11. Congruence

Congruence is that aspect of PUAs Game where his external state is congruent with his inner state. For example a PUA who is trying to show that he is an Alpha Male but internally feels very needy may be lacking authenticity in his behavior. Sometimes women use Shit Test to see if the PUA's inner state is really congruent (in agreement) with his external self.

7.12. Congruence Test

These tests are generally thrown out by women towards the PUA to check his inner confidence. These can be in the form of contradictory behavior or provocative comments made by women to see how the PUA handle the social pressure. It could be behavior like suddenly getting too close to the PUA or it could be suddenly asking some embarrassing question etc. PUAs usually learn to remain calm in these situations and not show signs of nervousness.

7.13. Compliance Test

Compliance Test is usually used by PUA to see if the target is showing interest in him. It can be done by asking for some simple approval (e.g. like moving over to another part of the club) or even by seeing how she responds to touching. Similarly Target women may also check compliance by asking for some favor like asking the PUA to buy her a drink. The most important thing that the PUA needs to remember is never to shows over-compliance as it can make him look needy and desperate. This will immediately create repulsion in women. The best way to pass a Compliance Test is by not complying with it, or asking for compliance from her in return.

7.14. Flirting

Flirting is not the same as simple rapport building. It is all about using humor to build a 'deeper' romantic (seductive) connection. PUAs develop skills of flirting by constant practice through trial and error. Also it is a way of gauging the targets compliance. Sometimes women may play hard to get or may be testing the PUA. In those situations learning to use Negging technique is helpful. You can learn more about flirting techniques by searching the Internet. Most important is to be funny and not too serious while flirting. Moreover you must remember that every person has a different style and sense of humor, so you need to develop your own unique style by constant practice.

7.15. Negging

PUAs use Negging or harmless sarcastic remarks, which are designed to break the woman's arrogance. It is not an insult but more like a backhand compliment. However if the woman has poor self-esteem then it can actually put her on the defense. However for over-confident snooty women it is a good way to break their resistance. Example "It's really cute how your nose wiggles when you talk - look, there it goes again...", "Those are interesting nails - are they real?"

7.16. Escalation

Escalation means taking the next step from rapport building to pick-up. PUAs do that after they have received at least three positive indications from the target. It can be done by Isolation, followed by Kino techniques.

7.17. Isolation

It means separating the target from the group and also providing her with a less pressured social environment away from her friends. It indicates the subconscious element of trust building. For example the PUA often would ask the woman to move to another part of the club that is quieter. This will prevent the Target from being interrupted by her other friends (Obstacles to the PUA). After Isolating the Target the PUA needs to escalate the Game.

7.18. Kino (Touching)

PUAs use Kino techniques to escalate from initial touch to sex. Kino stands for non-verbal means of communication. It needs to be very slow and gradual and can be started with handshakes, high fives, playful pushes, etc. It should begin with touching a woman in a non-threatening and non-sexual way on parts of the body that are non-intimate. As she gets more comfortable the PUAs takes it further. However if she appears to be not yet ready, then the PUA must slow down. This process is called Calibration of her response. This is done by constantly checking how compliant the woman is to the PUAs requests.

7.19. Group dynamics

PUA need to understand the dynamics of a target group of women before he can isolate the target woman. He can do that by befriending the whole group and increasing his social acceptability. Then he can work towards isolating the target woman. It is often easier to deal with groups of women if the PUA is with a Wing-man. In that case the Wing-man can engage the group while the PUA works on the Target. If there is a very active member in this group who can be an obstacle to the PUA, in that situation the Wing-man can help by distracting the obstacle while PUA works towards isolating the Target.

7.10. Cat String Theory

Cat string theory is based on the fact that women devalue things which come easily. They like the chase and therefore the PUA knows not to shower her with too much attention at the beginning of the pick-up. The name comes from the behavior of cats. A cat will chase after a feather that is dangled in front of it from a string, but will quickly lose interest in the feather if it is simply placed in front of the cat.

7.11. One on One (101) technique

This is a technique by which the PUA shows attention and then withdraws it from the Target. It is a way of being unpredictable. By doing this the PUA keeps the interest going in the Target. The PUAs knows that being predictable is boring to the target and therefore it is important to keep her interest alive by being unpredictable.

7.12. Role Reversal

The concept of reversing typical female and male gender roles during the Game is called Role Reversal. It is a great technique in building 101. In this the PUA uses scripts or phrases that are usually used by the women, example "I don't have sex on the first date, just so you know. I am only promising good conversation tonight." In these techniques the PUA can actually create sexual tension by showing that he is defending himself and the woman is trying to chase him.

7.13. Active Disinterest

PUAs use this method to deal with Hot Babes (women who are very beautiful and are aware of their influence on most men.) When dealing with such women the PUA continues active engagement with her but does not show any interest in her beauty. This can intrigue the beauty and want her to feel challenged by the PUA. This can result in her feeling more attracted to the PUA. In the end, it is human psychology to want the things that one can't have, and to pursue the things that are hard to get. For men and women, it is often the thrill of the chase that generates the most attraction.

7.14. Punish / Reward

This is another way of dealing with Hot Babe (HB) arrogant behavior. When she shows IOD, the PUA knows how to punish her negative behavior by using Negs. Similarly if she uses IOI then the PUA rewards her by encouraging with similar positive behavior. If the PUA punishes good behavior, he will first, possibly insult her, and second, discourage further good behavior. The art of Punish / Reward lies in unpredictability. If she continues with her negative behavior, the PUA knows to ignore her and continue focusing on another target.

7.15. Commonality

PUAs try to find commonalities with the target woman in order to build comfort and trust. However he does not agree with everything she says. Instead he build into the conversation some tension by disagreeing with her at times and finally reward and relate to make her feel like these commonalities are hard-won.

7.16. Reward & Relate (R&R)

The PUAs use R&R conversational technique to build rapport with the woman by mixing in Rewarding and Relating in conversations. He does this by genuinely listening to her, and then rewarding her with his own comments. This makes the target feel that the PUA is able to relate to her.

7.17. Becoming the Ideal Guy

Here is a good way to get into a woman's head (and with a bit of luck - pants later on). Ask her to describe her ideal guy. Ask for details. Ask about his hair, clothing, and height. Ask what kind of job he would have. Ask how he would talk, dress, behave. How would he smell? How would he touch you? If she is still into the Game, keep going. Ask how he would make love to her? What would he do to show his romantic side? Make mental notes and then use it as a guide to model that behavior. Also another good use of this type of conversation is that when she imagines this virtual man, she is getting hotter and hotter - and guess who is making her feel that way? That's you!

7.18. Conclusion

In the Middle Game in order to be successful, here are some essential tips.

- Don't be a puppy dog
- Be occasionally unpredictable
- Be interesting
- Talk slowly
- Be decisive
- Two steps forward, one step back
- Never ever be negative

Early on in the Game be in the Conversational Mode, in the Middle be in the Fun Mode and later on be in the Sexual Mode. Don't be in the wrong mode at the wrong time.

Chapter 8
Closing the Game

8.1. Introduction

Never spend time with a woman without some kind of closure - preferably a contact for a date. Closing means to complete a stage of the pick up game by getting a woman to commit to a "date", giving you her phone number, or bedding her literally on the spot. However most PUAs like to differentiate between different kinds of closes (Kiss Close, Number Close, Fuck Close, etc.) The term comes from sales terminology, i.e. "Close a deal". For the PUA the final deal is to get her to bed. It is not just about being friends. But the PUA must make sure that the target does not suspect his agenda. It should all appear spontaneous and natural.

8.2. Prior to Closing

The PUA has watched for cues, established rapport, touched appropriately, made a great impression on the target / group and gotten her off to the side in order to connect one on one. Now it's time to move into the next step: making the date. The rest falls into place from there.

8.3. First Close: Contact Close

Remember, first of all, that the Contact Close (Number Close) is merely a bridge to a future meet and nothing more. It is a logistical necessity, not the goal of the PUA. The PUA never begs for her number – instead he makes it sound mutual. After the PUA has gamed the Target successfully and is about to leave by showing some false time constraints, he can just transition into "What's the best number to reach you?" or "I'll call you tomorrow. Can you jot down your number?" If she refuses, the PUA lets her go but never beg as it will make him look desperate. If she asks for the PUAs number, he can pretend to look surprised and then find some reason not to give her. If she has the number, she will be the one in charge – not the PUA. Then the PUA would have to rely on the Target to contact him – it is a recipe for disaster! As an alternative to the phone number you can get her email or Facebook / Myspace contact info. Remember that a PUA needs to be the person in control. Phone call is always better because it shows confidence – texting is a sign of lack of confidence.

8.3.1. Calling / Emailing

Most PUAs as a rule contact the Target within 48 hours. Otherwise the Target will lose interest. It is better to call her than to send email. Using a calm relaxed voice over the phone shows that the PUA is in control. The PUA does that by preparing a script and talking slowly with pause to create a sense of confidence. He knows that without preparation he is likely to feel nervous. If you call her – remind her of your conversation – the funny bits of it to build rapport and also to stimulate her emotions. Continue with humorous chitchatting just to build up a deeper connection. If she is responding warmly, then ask her out. However be specific about the date & time and have a clear plan ready. Try to link it up with something she is interested in. Make it different from usual date – make it sound exciting and a new experience. Also make it on your own turf closer to your place so that you can make transition to bed easily. Have a back-up plan ready. Do not speak for more than 20 to 30 minutes and make sure you stay in control by deciding when to end the call. That will keep her wanting for more.

8.3.2. Leaving message on Answering Machine

If you have to leave a message on the answering machine, be prepared for what to say before you call. Leave a charming funny voice message saying that you will call back or leave your number so she can call you by when. Be specific otherwise she will think you are desperate. What if she does not call back? Call her two days later at a different time of the day and just leave a shorter message. Never ask why she did not call. Then move on.

8.4. Second Close: Priming Date

Priming date is the first date. It should be brief – maximum one and half hour. It is all about building familiarity and getting to know each other better. It needs to be in simple place and not too fancy. It is important to look good and also appear busy. Carrying a book is a good idea – especially if it is on a topic of common interest. Also it is important to reach the venue earlier.

8.4.1. Top Places for Exciting Priming Dates

Priming Dates are inexpensive and yet need to be fun and exciting.

Example: Amusement parks, Art galleries, Beaches, Bike rides, Boating, Comedy clubs, Concerts, Cooking classes, Festivals, Fireworks display, Museums, Parks/nature hikes, Picnics, Planetariums/Aquariums, Salsa lessons, Shopping, Sporting events, Theater, Wine tasting, Yoga class, Zoos

8.4.2. Bad places for Priming dates

Arcades, Car shows, Dangerous locations, Horrific / violent movies, Movie theaters, Nudist resorts, Out with buddies, Overnight trips, Places where old girlfriends work, Places with lots of single men (competition!), Sporting events (if she does not like them!), Sports bars (if she does not like them!), Strip clubs, Video stores

8.4.3. If she doesn't turn up

Be prepared because it will happen at times. PUAs never take these things personally. Hang around for 15 minutes and if you still do not hear from her – just leave. At times PUAs can use an unusual strategy to turn the table on her. They may call her later – say after an hour and apologize for missing the date. They can also use some story to emphasize that they were busy / stuck up. If she did miss the date innocently, this gives her another chance to make up. Also the PUA needs to be confident when pulling this routine so that he does not sound anxious or desperate.

8.4.4. What to talk about

PUAs go prepared with a list of questions – usually romantic emotional themes are good. Also it is good to use story to introduce sexual topics. Follow up emotional or sensual topics by asking her about her opinion. Ask her personal questions about her preferences like how she likes to be kissed, things that are most romantic for her, what impresses her, what turns her on etc. While talking use soft suggestive words like – seduce, sensual, erotic, attraction, exotic, romance, passion etc. Collect as much information about her emotional needs so that you can use them at a later date.

8.4.5. Sensuous Seduction Date

This is the second stage where the PUA works on escalating things to a more intimate physical level. This date is usually three or more hours in duration. The place needs to be something exciting and exotic. Combine entertainment, dinner, little dancing, quite ride, last drink – may be a stop over at your place at the end. Pay for everything if you want to impress her and plan to take her to bed. If after all the intimate conversation it will really backfire if you try to split the bill! Please be realistic!

8.4.6. How to get her to your Place

- Have her drive over and meet you at your place, then take your car to the rest of the date. She has to come back to get her car.

- Offer to show her something you have that she might be interested in i.e. music collection, art pieces, fantastic city view and so on.
- Meet her at the lobby of your place, and then conveniently forget something upstairs like your credit card or whatever.
- Offer her dessert at your house and make it real dessert.
- If it's late, offer to let her sleep over - her in your bed and YOU on the couch.

8.4.7. How to make her feel Special

Arrive early and wait outside for her. Give her your best smile and a gentle hug. If you haven't kissed her yet, don't do it now. Create a sense of romance by giving her a small gift that would suit her personality. Use the information you have collected about her during the Priming Date. Make her feel surprised – which the essence of romance. Wrap the gift beautifully – these things show her that you have thought of her. Add a card which makes her feel that you value her presence. Do not try to flatter her – that would make her feel you are needy. Some gift ideas include – Books, Chocolate, Massage oil, Music CD, Scented soaps, Stuffed animals, Unusual pen etc.

8.4.8. Kino Escalation (KE)

KE means physically escalating with the woman, from the initial touch to sex. It starts by casual quick touch over non-intimate areas (within her comfort zone) in a non-sexual way (e.g. hand shakes, high fives, playful pushes, etc.). Make good relaxed eye contact and may be wink at her during the conversation. Scan her from head to toe once in a desirable appreciative way – but not in a threatening way. Monitor her response. Slowly build up the escalation. Complement her on her strengths to make her feel good – two to three times at the most. If she is very beautiful, complement some other aspect of her but not her beauty. As the woman grows accustomed to the touch, you can then escalate to more intimate parts of the woman's body, starting with the legs, then the torso, and finally the face and hair. From there, it is only a small step to go in for a kiss and move into direct sexual escalation. While the above is a slow progression for Kino escalation, it is possible to skip steps along the process and jump directly into more intimate forms of Kino, depending on the woman's attraction for the PUA and also her compliance levels. For example, it is possible to get into a sexual state and immediately go in for a kiss, without having previously established any Kino. Making such a jump requires calibration of her response. Otherwise it will result in a blow out.

8.4.9. Calibration

Calibration means constantly checking her response and adjusting the Game. PUAs use calibration to be flexible in his strategy to Game the Target depending on circumstances rather than sticking to a rigid approach.

8.5. Third Close: Kiss Close (K-Close)

The first kiss with the target is important for the women. The PUA needs to make her feel special and not like a slut. The kiss is not the end game for the PUA. So the PUA needs to be selective about where he K-Closes, be gentle with his kisses, and only sexually escalate to a make out in a private location. Never ask her if you can kiss her – just do it. During the seduction date look for opportunity to kiss her – may be when dancing or even when she is relaxed and laughing. Make it appear spontaneous. You can even be playful by slowly leading up to it. Come close and back away. Rest your forehead on hers and share breath. Go forward to kiss her and deviate to her neck or ear. Ask her "Do you want to kiss me?" or lean in close, sigh and say, "I am trying so hard not to kiss you right now." If things are going well and you have been reading all of her signs correctly, chances are she will either lean forward to kiss you and / or pull you towards her. Never talk about other women or say that you have been planning (reading PUA books); just make her feel that everything is spontaneous and you are just living in the moment and because you find her so irresistible. …that is why all this is happening! Also do not be indecisive once you approach her – be slow and gentle. Never thank her after the kiss as it will make you sound desperate. If she refuses – never beg or argue. Wait and calibrate till she is ready. By the way make sure that you smell good and your teeth are clean.

8.5.1. Proceeding

Ask yourself is she ready for sex yet or does she need more preparation? If she needs more priming then schedule a third date shortly and this time offer to invite her to your place (on your own turf). Say that you would make dinner for her because you are a creative cook! Most women appreciate men who can cook - so even if you cannot – just get some exotic takeaway and pretend that you made it. Create the atmosphere with dim lights, candle, romantic music, champagne and some dessert. Cooking for a woman often makes her feel very special. It can be a sensual experience that makes you appear even more competent and attractive than before.

8.5.2. Progression

At last, it's time to make that next move - the one that leads from a long kiss to that horizontal rumba. Suggest that you head someplace quieter, more private, cooler / warmer where you both can be more comfortable. It can be out for a cup of coffee or going for a nice, long walk - where the two of you can be alone together. From there, your kisses should turn passionate and because it's clear to you that this woman is not interested in stopping. Hands begin to roam, the body temperature goes up and as quickly as possible you two are headed for the bed. A first meeting that ends in Sex - it's the best close of all and the one that lets you know that you sure know how to G-close with women.

8.5.3. Sexual State

Getting into a Sexual State is a powerful way to shift from the comfort phase to seduction to actual sex. Transitioning into this state / mode means communicating by body language (non-verbal way) to the woman that you want to have sex. It involves lowering one's energy level, slowing down one's voice tone, and looking at the woman in a seductive, almost hungry manner. The best way to convey the Sexual State is to actually be in it. If the woman is at all interested, she will follow the PUA's lead, and also enter into a Sexual State. From there the PUA can go in for a passionate kiss and escalate sexually (assuming he is in a proper location for sex). An advanced PUA will often be able to start off an interaction already in a sexual state. This serves the purpose of screening out women who are not immediately interested in sex, and can lead to instant sex.

8.6. Fuck Close or Full Close

Means completing a 'pick-up' by having sex with the Target. It is the ultimate goal of the PUA.

8.7. Girl Close (G-Close)

A G (Girl) Close is what happens when the PUA Contact Close (number or email or both) a Target and it leads to a F (Full/Fuck) Close rather than a flake or lets just be friends (LJBF). G-Closing also happens when you Fuck Close the same-day. The concept is simple. Rather than thinking "I would like to get with that chick, how am I going to get her phone number?" you must be thinking, "What should I be doing to get her to want to fuck me?" You're talking to a chick you just met. If all you're thinking about is contact closing her to follow up later, you may very well get her number or email. But you'll probably get a flake. A Contact Close is not a guarantee of anything except yet another speed bump on the road to laying her. If you get her number but don't get her imagining fucking you, you are only making your job harder. Get her to want to fuck you when you first meet her. Then if you contact close, the follow up is more promising. Close the target first, not her contact info - this is the Direct Game approach of advanced PUAs.

Chapter 9
Progression to Sex

9.1. Introduction

The time has finally come for having sex. You have been working on developing rapport, value and comfort with several different women. You've gone on a few dates with each one. It's time to transition from heavy foreplay to the real thing. Before we discuss the ways you can get that Hot Babe (HB) into your hot bed, we want to make two things very clear from the very start. _Remember that sex has to be consensual; otherwise she may file a case against you for rape. Also use condoms because it is safe and prevents you from sexual diseases and child support payments._

9.2. The Female Mind on Sex

When it comes to sex, male and females think differently.

All women are very concerned about their reputation and do not want to be branded as sluts. Also they tend to worry excessively about being hurt or becoming pregnant. In short most women are cautious and not as impatient to have sex as men are. It is the PUAs job to help her deal with her concerns and apprehensions. You can do that by creating trust and making her feel comfortable with you. You want her to think of your place as a fun, relaxed place to be. Make sure that your house or apartment is neat and clean with the bed made. Dim the lights and leave some soft, sexy music on before you leave the house.

9.3. Break State

A Break State is a sudden change in the context of conversation or feeling which shows a shift in the targets motivation to go ahead with sex. This happens to most women. Suddenly your target may feel the need to back out. This is due to Last Minute Resistance and the PUA needs to be prepared to deal with this.

9.4. Last Minute Resistance (LMR)

LMR is the resistance that a woman puts up to physical advances before sex. It causes a woman to freeze up before having sex. She usually puts up LMR to physical advances when sex is imminent. This usually takes the form of the woman resisting having their bra or panties taken off, or putting up any other sort of resistance to impede the PUA. Dealing with LMR often starts early in the interaction, using comfort building, and slowing down the interaction to assure the woman that the PUA is interested in more than just sex, and that they will stick around after the physical act. Other ways of dealing with LMR include using Freeze Outs and just pure persistence. If you want to get laid, you had better prepare for LMR ahead of time. It takes a combination of avoidance, blurring and distraction techniques. *Avoidance* means the PUA takes every possible step to prevent State Change from happening in the first place. ***Blurring*** means lessening the intensity of the State Change. ***Distraction*** means getting the woman's attention onto something else so they forget about the shift.

9.5. State Change / Shift

A change in the target's emotions and mindset at any given situation due to LMR.

9.5.1. First State Change

The First State Change can take place when you transition from wherever you went on your date to your house. This is the point where she thinks to herself, that he plans to seduce me when he gets me into his place. I had better be on guard. For some women, they are already preparing their objections in their minds. Using avoidance - you have prepared this shift to be easy by making sure your place looks nice and romantic and she is having a great time with you. Using blurring - if she gets uncomfortable walking into your place, make sure it is close to where you already were so it's a smooth transition. Stop by your place to pick up a jacket or show her the photographs you had been telling her about earlier. This blurs the reason you are there. Using distraction - walk in and offer her a drink, start a fire, put on some music - anything that makes her focus on something other than waiting for you to grab her.

9.5.2. Second State Change

The Second State Change is when you move her from the couch to the bedroom. You are already sitting together on the couch because you made sure the chairs were holding other things like pillows (avoidance). You may end up having sex on the couch because it flows right and feels natural, or you may head to another room. If she protests, you slow down (blurring) and back off a bit. If she pulls back, you refresh her drink or turn up the music (distraction).

9.5.3. Third State Change

The Third State Change is when you take her clothing off. This is an awkward moment for her. You most likely will never begin to imagine how self-conscious women are about their bodies. So make taking off her clothes a sensual and smooth experience (avoidance). This is a good time to throw in a few compliments about how she look's, but be respectful. "Wow, you're really beautiful," not "wow, great tits." Be knowledgeable about how bras work. Don't fumble; unsnap it in one motion. Kiss her on the neck or across the abdomen or lower back as you take off her shirt and bra (distraction). Take her underwear off along with her pants or skirt, so it is only one motion (blurring). Take time to compliment parts of her body but look beyond the obvious. Tell her that her skin is so soft, her eyes sparkle, her hair is like silk, etc. It may sound corny to you but say it sincerely and she will love it.

9.5.4. Fourth State Change

The Fourth State Change is one of the toughest to do smoothly but practice will help (avoidance). Slip the condom on. You can do it while you are kissing her elsewhere (blurring) and then move into her most erogenous areas (distraction) like her boobs or clit (a definite distraction). Remember, many women find their boobs more erogenous than their clit, so don't ignore the boobs!

9.5.6. Fifth State Change

The Fifth State Change is penetration. If a woman is ready for this moment, it will happen naturally and smoothly. She will welcome it. If she is not ready, this can be startling and a definite state changer. It may feel invasive. To make sure it is a pleasant experience, you need to ensure she is wet (avoidance) for easy sliding (either through plain old arousal or oral sex), be touching her elsewhere at that moment (blurring) and whisper to her or call out her name (distraction).

9.6. Overcoming Her Objections

It's important that you listen carefully to the woman you are with to see if she is giving you a 'token' objection or a real one. The difference is this: a token objection is one that she feels she has to make or she will come across like a slut. She doesn't want to be easy, so she has to try and slow down things when they start to escalate. A token objection is one in which she says something along the lines of, "Should we really be doing this already?" but she keeps kissing, touching, rubbing and licking. By making a small protest, she is convincing herself that she is not really doing anything shameful . . . she tried to stop but was seduced! If she does say something like this, then back off a little. If you were under her skirt, go back to under her shirt. Whatever step you were at, just go back one step. Stay there a while and then try the next step again. She may very well go right along with it this time. On the other hand, a "Real" objection is when she pushes you away and says, "No! I am not ready for this!" That means STOP. Going further against her wish means rape!

9.7. The Freeze Out

The deliberate but casual ignoring of the target woman is called Freeze Out. If she tells you to stop and you are not sure if this was a token or real objection, test it. Say 'okay' - cheerfully. This is no big deal for you. Turn up the lights, straighten your clothing and go do something else. Go in the kitchen and get something to eat. Check your email. Pull out the chess or checkers game. Find something neutral - as well as boring - to do. See what happens. If she goes with it, she meant no. If she comes over and re-initiates romance, follow it and go back to where you were. It was just a token. Freezing out will take away the good Kino feelings, making her want it back. It is important not to be angry or overly emotional during a Freeze Out, or draw much attention to it at all, which would come across as spiteful or needy.

9.8. Reverse Psychology

One of the best ways to overcome an objection is one of Reverse Psychology. If she says, "I am not having sex with you," then you can respond with, "Who said we were going to do that anyway? I'm just enjoying touching you." To take it even one step further, when she says something along the lines of, "We are moving too fast. I am not ready for this," pull back, think a moment and then say, in a gentle but serious tone, "You're probably right. Maybe we should wait. I think you are worth it." You would not believe how many women respond to this by jumping on you. You've affirmed their feelings and told them that you like them enough to just hold off, as difficult as it may be and that is often a huge turn on.

9.9. Overcoming the Age Objection

If you are younger than the woman you are with, it is rare to have age as a problem (unless she perceives you as immature). Older women often truly appreciate a younger man. They are flattered by your attention and probably adore your stamina. If the girl you are seducing, however, is younger than you are, she may be concerned about having an 'older' lover - even if that means you are just a few years older than she is. You could lie. But it takes way too much effort to maintain them. If she asks about your age (never volunteer the info), tell her the truth. If she seems offset by it, demonstrate the many reasons she does not need to be. Reassure her that your age has given you time to learn some important life lessons that you can show her. Your age doesn't make you old - it makes you experienced and skilled. She should be grateful to have a lover that knows what he is doing. Turn her negative statement into a positive one.

9.10. Five Easy Ways to Overcome LMR:

Last Minute Resistance like "We should wait" or "We shouldn't do this." are common. So relax and be calm. Here are the tips:

1. Make sure she is significantly turned on. The first time you have sex with a new woman; make sure you spend twice as much time during foreplay. An easy trick is to make her cum one time first with either oral sex or by fingering her to near climax…then as she's begging you to fuck her, give her what she wants.

2. Make sure she knows you'll still respect her in the morning. One of the main reasons girls make guys wait is because she's unsure if you'll still respect her in the morning, and more importantly still want to see her again. Easy ways to let a girl know you'll still respect her even after having sex include, making a date for next week. Talk about it before you get into bed, and then

reconfirm your date while in foreplay.

3. Agree with everything she says: no matter what! Never ever, argue with a girl during sex. Bringing her mind back into logic is the worst thing you can do to kill the mood. So instead, just agree with her and turn her on even more.

4. Make sure you have all four elements of the D.E.V.I. Model – Dominance (taking lead), Emotion (connecting emotionally), Variety (using sexual technique variations like oral sex, erotic massage etc.) and Immersion (concentrating on giving her pleasure)

5. Try and try again, but know when to take second place. The first time a girl says "we shouldn't," consider it a reflex, if she says it again, most likely it is what we call token resistance. The first two "no"s don't mean much, and should be expected, especially if the "no"s are "we shouldn't." Keep moving forward, turning her on and getting her more in the mood. Or if she resists, take a step

back and move to a different part of her body to turn her on. A third "no" however, could very well mean not today.

Note: One PUA reports that he simply tells her "Sweetie, you turned me on so much that I really need to cum….if you're not ready to have sex today, it's okay, but I'm going to have to relieve myself at least." He says "I've actually done this many times with many different girls, because I realized that it feels almost just as good to have a girl give you a blow job, hand job, or even just kiss your neck and rub her tits on you while you jack yourself off. Afterwards you'll both feel more sexually bonded and chance are you'll end up having sex with her sooner than later because you didn't get angry."

9.11. Conclusion

Final Advice: Whatever you do, just remember; don't get angry at yourself or at her. Last Minute Resistance is normal and there are always ways around it. We hope you remember these tips the next time you're in this situation.

Chapter 10

Miscellaneous Topics

10.1. Sex with Cheating Women

As a PUA, you are a hunter – you are looking for sexual recreation. If it happens that you end up with some woman who is cheating on her partner that is necessarily her choice. If she is cheating, out of guilt she may try to put all the responsibility on the PUA. So as a PUA it is important to be prepared to deal with it. She may try to tell you that her relationship is great and you are spoiling it. Do not take it personally. You may find that she is making efforts to bring you together with her Partner. In front of the partner she is showing that she is very loyal, but when her partner is not there, she may continue to flirt with the PUA. She may even share with you (the PUA) the fact that she is cheating on her partner. Actually when women are in relationship, they are not hit by men as often – and this in turn often lowers her self-esteem.

That is why she may be looking towards you to boost her self-esteem. You can ask her casually – is you partner really treating you the way you deserve to be treated? Most women will start thinking seriously about these issues if you can plant a seed of doubt in her mind. Do not criticize the partner directly – instead subtly point out certain issues about her partner or relationship and keep planting doubts – then you can reap the benefits sooner than later.

10.2. Becoming a Good Lover

In order to become a good PUA you have not only got to perfect the Pick-Up Art but also become a Good Lover. You can become that by making an emotional connection with the target. For women emotional connection is important part of sexual connection. Spend time in foreplay and get her ready – the hornier she gets the easier it will be for you to become a good lover. Be aware of her sensitive parts of the body and when playing with her look at her eyes in a seductive way. Progress slowly and take your time - the slower the better for her, complement her by encouraging her and rewarding her when she tries to please you. Make her cum first by using oral sex or fingers etc. After-play is also very important for women – so continue to cuddle and kiss her and talk to her seductively even after the orgasm for at least ten minutes before you get up. Never talk about other women during sex, she will get turned off. A good lover is somebody who is very caring, is aware of their lovers needs and is not just thinking about their own pleasure. They will go that extra step to ensure that their partner is fully satisfied even if this means that they are participating in something that they do not really want to and that they might not even enjoy. A good lover will not pressure their partner into doing something that they do want to. Otherwise this will lead to a lot of resentment in the future. A good lover will make the whole experience of making love into a romantic one, roses on the bed, candles and champagne etc. These extra measures can lead to extra pleasures! Good lovers will at times tease their partner by moving in a slow manner however at other times will become dominant and quick. Having sex in unusual places rather than just in the bedroom can also prove to be exciting and different. A good lover will also like to try out many different sexual positions to ensure that sex does not become boring. In conclusion, variety is the key to sexual satisfaction for you and your lover.

10.3. Svengali Challenge

It is a PUA term for the simple challenge issued to all those men who are not getting enough women and sex and blame themselves. Get out of your nest and become socially active. Start smiling / saying "Hi" to all women you come across. If you are able to do that then you have enough skills to begin the PUA journey. However if you find it hard then you are not suited to become a PUA. This is a test for your own social skills.

10.4. Dos and Don'ts for PUAs

Don'ts

- Don't beg in order to gain the desire / respect of a woman. Let her put in equal effort.
- Don't reduce your value and let her walk over you.
- Don't hesitate to playfully disagree and tease her. She's a human being with flaws & issues just like everybody else.
- Don't tell a girl too much about how you feel early on in the relationship.
- Don't talk to her on the phone / IM program for hours on end. Always show that you are busy.
- Don't over-analyze everything she does or says. If you can't tell if she's into you, then most likely she's not.
- Don't try to change her mind about you if she is not interested.
- Don't ask her what movie she wants to see or

where she wants to have dinner. Take control and make the decisions yourself.

- Don't go overly out of your way to do things for her. Act to her as you'd act to a friend in regards to favors. Treat her as a human being, not a Goddess!

- Don't be afraid to rip her clothes off, bend her over a lounge & pound the shit out of her every once in awhile - just as long as she feels safe with you.

Dos

- Do act confidently at all times after you have grabbed her attention. Be comfortable in your own skin.

- Do be busy with other things in life. Believe in the Supply & Demand theory – let her enjoy chasing you. Give her the gift of missing you.

- Do show that you are interested in being her lover but not just friends.

- Do learn to read her body language and indicators

of interest.

- Do let her do most of the talking. When she asks you questions, be funny / witty and keep your answers shorter. Only answer maybe half of the question she asked. This is how you stay, 'mysterious".

- Do always remember that there are other women out there, just as attractive, cute and cool as the one you're dealing with now. Treat all Targets (women) as replaceable.

- Do show your feelings with actions, not words.

- Do escalate physically when you feel like it. Not when you think she feels like it.

10.5. Ten Important Steps to Becoming a PUA

1. Read PUA Secrets repeatedly. It is a well-organized Beginner's manual. Seriously! Reading too many different books will only confuse you. Main thing is to understand the key concepts and

try them out in real time.

2. Never use other peoples routines directly, improvise and make it your own.

3. Make going out a habit. The more the better – but at least two or three times every week. Becoming a PUA is like learning an instrument; you have to practice to get good at it.

4. Get some hot female friends - you can use your new female friends as pivots, and most importantly, they will introduce you to other women. It's a win-win situation.

5. Get involved in the local PUA community through Internet search. Then go out Sarging (hunting Targets) with them – be a Wing-man for others to begin with.

6. Go out alone at times. You need to learn how to play the Game alone, without a Wing-man, otherwise you will always be dependent on other person which is something you should strongly avoid.

7. Focus on building a big social circle including men – and women. Pick-up should only be one of many aspects of your life. PUA is a lifestyle, but you will miss out on a lot of nice things if it is the only thing you do.

8. Develop your own style and look after your physical appearance

9. Work on overall personal development including your finances, your relationships with friends / parents / neighbors, your car, your apartment etc.

10. Figure out what you really want – are you looking for the ideal woman to have a long term relationship or do you want just more sex with more women. Then go after it and don't waste your time on anything that will not get you the results you REALLY want.

10.6. Seven Great Places for PUA Hunting

These are some of the places where we PUAA have

found more women for Picking Up. Some are common places with lots of women but more competition, and then some really uncommon but higher quality women.

 # 7: Bars & Nightclubs: Bars are not the best places, but single lonely women drinking alone are often waiting to be picked up – although not the best women. With nightclubs, on particular nights and during the "rush hours" they're packed with girls who are there to get hooked up. Plus, you can pickup more than one girl per evening out. Choose your spot correctly beforehand - the busiest spot at the bar – lots of women will be cramming to get past you as they try to order their drinks in the chaos. You'll get a constant series of perfect moments, for opening conversations with the girls of your choice!

 # 6: Mega Shopping Mall: Women love to shop. Choose your time. Find the best spots where women tend to congregate. Try the lunch-break, after work, and later in the evening. Then pick the time, frequented by the kind of women you would like to meet!

 # 5: *Fragrance Stores:* These are the places that sell bath oils, shower gels, body lotions. Women can't get enough of this stuff.

 # 4: *Franchise Coffee Shops:* After a long, "tough" day of shopping, women love to drop all their bags and relax with a coffee / tea. They're bored, they're tired, and they'd just love some company. Try asking her if her shopping adventure was successful - then be prepared to spend the next hour reviewing her collection.

 # 3: *Franchise Bookstores:* Especially on "dating nights" and weekends, when a women who doesn't have a date that week, can easily occupy herself for an entire evening, book-browsing. Choose your books. In every section that women frequent, pick one book (preferably a new best-seller) and when you see a girl you'd like to know better - you've got something to talk about.

 # 2: Clothing Stores: Hot women spend a ton of time shopping for clothes. As long as you know a bit about the "latest" in woman's fashions, you're good to go. You're there, looking for a gift for your sister (or your cousin, or your niece - someone around her age). Do you think that maybe, that cute girl you just walked up to, could help you find the right gift?

 # 1: Health Food Stores: Health food stores have some of the best looking women as customers. You can bet there will be great-looking women going there. Try the after-work rush.

These are the some of the easy-to-find, easy-to-use, pickup locations. But there are always more places.... you need to find out by going out regularly and playing the Game.

10.7. The Fast Track to Emotional Connection

1. Give the woman the feeling she has known you for much longer than she has – make her feel comfortable with you.

2. If, when you do approach her, it is obvious that she is not definitely interested then let it go immediately. Good PUAs do not waste time flogging dead horses.

3. Every good PUA know: what you say is less important than how you say it. Be spontaneous, natural and confident. Don't think too much about what impression you are creating on the Target as this will make you feel anxious.

10.8. Four Essential Qualities Women Want in Men

1. A Life of their Own, not needy but independent
2. Confidence and relaxed under pressure
3. Intelligent with good communication skills
4. Sense of humor

10.9. How important are looks in Men?

What women want in Men - are physical looks important? Attraction works very differently in women than it does in men. A guy's attractiveness towards women comes more from his personality. The men who emit confidence, are challenging, and show other Alpha Male qualities are inherently attractive. If they have good looks then it is an additional benefit. If you can display enough of these traits and know how to communicate them properly to any woman you will be able to get into her pants in no time.

1. Ambition (Goal or direction)
2. Emotionally Stable (not needy)
3. High Social Value (humor)

10.10. Five Mistakes AFCs Make

1. Being too needy and dependent
2. Trying too hard
3. Being sheepish or wussy
4. Bragging or trying to be someone different
5. Lack of direction in life.

These are all signs of insecurity and lack of self-confidence. These repel women – women only want men they can respect.

10.11. Advice for Beginners

Being a PUA is about being a man who's successful with many women (sexually) and confident & comfortable with who he is.

1. Select a style of seduction that suits your personality. Once you've become more skilled and experienced, start experimenting with other styles.
2. Increase your knowledge by reading more books and articles on the subject including human

psychology, body language, and socializing.

3. Be Wing-man for experienced PUAs. For this you need to join your local PUA society (e.g. through Internet based forums)

4. Continue with your mission privately. Do not let everyone know as they may discourage you.

5. Keep trying continually the different things you have learned from the book.

6. Set realistic goals and praise yourself for every little progress you make.

7. Do not be afraid of setbacks. Everyone has setbacks. Those who succeed are the ones that handle the setbacks better than others, so if you fall on your face, brush yourself off and try again.

8. Always remain positive and make learning fun and enjoyable by going out with similar minded PUAs.

9. There is no short cut, instant success formula.

10. Increase you communication skills with women by talking to them whenever you get a chance.

10.12. Identifying Easy Targets

How do you identify the Easy Target from the prude or the cock-tease?

- Watch the Eyes - the easy Target stares at your eyes, your arms and your…other parts.
- Watch for women hanging out by the bar, sucking down booze, and enjoying male attention.
- Watch for a single woman chatting with many guys – she is seeking companionship.
- Watch for bright red lips at a nightclub.
- Watch for arguing women at the nightclub – one of them will be slut.
- Watch for body piercing particularly any piercing of the tongue.
- Watch the woman who smokes.
- Watch for Tattoos – may be she will show you her tattoo proudly.
- Watch to see if the tips of nipples are protruding

147

from under her dress.

- Watch the hands movements – particularly if she keeps touching your arm and your chest while talking to you!

Example: A woman with tattoos, cigarettes, red lips, a bellybutton ring, and a shot of whiskey who keeps touching you while yakking – she is the one for tonight.

10.13. Checklist for PUAs (Pick-up Algorithm)

Here are the basics for the Beginners in the form of a checklist that you can use or modify to suit your style. Go through the checklist whenever you are playing the Game – you will start winning sooner than later. Ask yourself these self-evaluating questions:

1. Have you got the looks and feel of a confident PUA?
2. Have you got a plan to open up the

conversation casually?

3. Are you flirting with her?

4. Are you making her feel comfortable with you?

5. Are you connecting with her by talking about common issues?

6. Are you giving her Kino stimulus?

7. Have you complemented her personality to make her feel good? (Do not overdo!)

8. Have you closed the deal with contact info?

Final Thoughts

This book is essentially for the Beginner level PUA. It will help you to get started easily as it gives you a clear structure for the Game. In terms of reading about different PUA styles, there is an overwhelming amount of Seduction material available both offline and online. It is important to begin applying them. Just reading is not of any use. We as experienced PUAs do believe that if you have reasonable social skills you can become a PUA. However there is no alternative to trial and error. No-one can expect to become a champion player overnight. Read as much as is healthy for you. But more important is to try it out, and keep what works for you. In this book we have given you all the core concepts that should give you a strong foundation. As you get more experienced, you will find out what work best for you and fits your personality and style. All PUAs constantly focus on improving their Game. Learn what your strongest attractive qualities are and accentuate them; identifying and eliminating the unattractive qualities, to make yourself a better Player. Learn the skills of communicating these attractive qualities to women, in as natural and efficient manner as possible. Never try to be someone else by copying their style directly – because our experience says it does not work that way. Be confident in your own skin because only that seems to work best. No method is perfect – the best method is what works for you!

Happy Sarging (hunting Targets) – and more SEX with more Women!

REQUEST FOR FEEDBACK

Dear Reader,

We value your Feedback.

On behalf of the authors we would like to listen to your comments. We are continuously trying to improve the self-help training products created by us to suit the needs of beginners. Our purpose is to generate **Easy** and **Effective training material** which can cater to the requirements of those who are new to the Game.

We would request you to give your comments about this book on its web-page by using the *'Customer Review'* section.

Please tell us what you thought of the product as this will help us and possibly other customers as well. We will apply your suggestions to create improved products in future to suit your particular requirements.

Your Satisfaction is our Inspiration.

Thank you.

Publisher